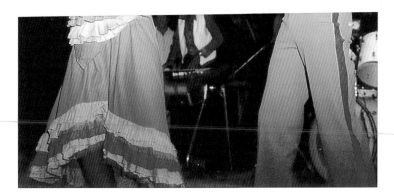

Linda Illsley

Books

Series editor: Polly Goodman
Book editor: Alex Edmonds
Designer: Mark Whitchurch
Cover design: Hodder Wayland
Picture researcher: Paula Chapman

First published in 1998 by Wayland Publishers Ltd.
This paperback, revised and updated edition published in 2006 by Hodder Wayland,
an imprint of Hodder Children's Books.
© Copyright 2006 Hodder Wayland

British Library Cataloguing in Publication Data
Illsley, Linda
The Caribbean. – 2nd ed. – (Festivals and food)
1. Cookery, Caribbean – Juvenile literature 2. Festivals –
Caribbean Area – Juvenile literature 3. Food habits –
Caribbean Area – Juvenile literature 4. Caribbean Area –
Social life and customs – Juvenile literature
I. Title II. Illsley, Linda. Flavour of the Caribbean
641.5'9729

ISBN-10: 0 7502 4839 4
ISBN-13: 978-0-7502-4839-6

Cover photograph: Selling fruit on a market stall in Jamaica.
Title page: Traditional dancers in Jamaica.
Contents page: Drinking the sweet milk of a coconut.

Photograph and artwork acknowledgements
Andes Press Agency 5 (top right), 7 (top); Axiom Photographic Agency 5 (middle left),
5 (middle right), 8, 9 (bottom); Eye Ubiquitous 5 (bottom right), 11, 13, 27 (Mike Alkins);
Robert Harding 9 (top); John and Penny Hubley 14 (top); Hutchinson Library 3, 23 (bottom)
(Eric Ayrs); Impact 7 (bottom), 24; James Davis title page, 10 (bottom), 17; Norton Studios,
Trinidad 28; Panos 5 (top left), 6, 12 (top); Betty Press 20; South American Pictures 21;
St Lucia Tourist Board 16, 26 (bottom); Trip 22 (T. Bogna), 12 (bottom) (A. Tovey);
Zul Mukhida 14 (bottom), 18, 26 (top). Fruit and vegetable artwork is by Tina Barber.
Map artwork on page 4 is by Hardlines. Step-by-step recipe artwork is by Judy Stevens.

Printed and bound in China

Hodder Children's Books
a division of Hodder Headline Limited
338 Euston Road, London NW1 3BH

CONTENTS

The Caribbean and its Food

The Caribbean

The Caribbean's place in the world

N

United States

ATLANTIC OCEAN

Nassau

BAHAMAS

Havana

CUBA

TURKS and
CAICOS ISLANDS

GREATER ANTILLES

CAYMAN ISLANDS

DOMINICAN
REPUBLIC

HAITI

LEEWARD ISLANDS

VIRGIN
ISLANDS

PUERTO
RICO

ANGUILLA

BARBUDA

Kingston

JAMAICA

HISPANIOLA

St CROIX

St KITTS and NEVIS

MONTSERRAT

SABA

ANTIGUA

GUADELOUPE

LESSER ANTILLES

DOMINICA

MARTINIQUE

CARIBBEAN SEA

St LUCIA

BARBADOS

0   400 km

0   200 miles

DUTCH
ANTILLES

ARUBA

WINDWARD ISLANDS

St VINCENT and
the GRENADINES

GRENADA

TOBAGO

TRINIDAD

SOUTH AMERICA

4

SUGAR CANE
Sugar cane was introduced to the Caribbean by European settlers. The juice of the sugar cane is used to make sugar, rum and a refreshing, sweet soft drink.

RICE
Rice is grown all over the Caribbean. It is one of many different foods which were brought to the Caribbean by Indian settlers.

FRUIT AND NUTS
The hot, Caribbean climate means that many different tropical fruits can be grown on the islands.

VEGETABLES
Root vegetables, such as yams and sweet potatoes, are an important part of the Caribbean diet. They were brought to the Caribbean from Africa.

FISH AND SEAFOOD
The Caribbean Sea is rich in fish and seafood, such as lobsters and crabs. Fish is cooked in many different ways.

SPICES
Ginger, nutmeg, peppers and allspice are grown in the Caribbean. They add flavour to many Caribbean dishes.

People, Food and Farming

▼ Once sugar cane has been harvested, it goes to factories to have the sweet juice crushed out of it.

The Caribbean is a region made up of over 30 large islands in the Caribbean Sea, between North and South America. It is in the tropics, so the climate is warm all year.

The people of the Caribbean are a mixture of many different cultures. The first people to live there were Arawak Indians. Then, 500 years ago, people from Spain, England, France and Holland settled in the Caribbean. They brought slaves from Western Africa to work on sugar and tobacco plantations. More recently, East Indians, Chinese and Arabs have settled there.

Each of these groups of people brought with them their traditional celebrations, their cooking and sometimes even the ingredients, which became part of the diet of Caribbean people.

Rice and bread

Rice and bread are very important in the Caribbean. Rice is used in dishes such as rice and peas, and with Indian curries and Chinese dishes.

Rice grows well in the tropical Caribbean climate because it needs rain and sunshine to grow. During most of the year the temperature stays between 25°C and 30°C and there is a rainy season between September and November.

There are lots of different types of bread in the Caribbean, but the most famous is the *dhalpourri*. This is a flat Indian bread made with ground split peas. It is filled with curried potatoes, meat, and chickpeas, and is rolled up and eaten like a sandwich.

▲ A rice harvest in Cuba.

Once rice has ▶ been picked, it is sieved to get rid of the husks, or shells, around each grain.

7

Tropical fruits

Caribbean people buy their fruit from large open markets. Some of the fruits, such as bananas, coconuts and mangoes, are sold abroad to countries like Britain.

Coconuts are very popular in the Caribbean. The 'milk' or juice inside is a refreshing drink and the kernel itself is used as an ingredient in many different dishes such as cakes, curries, sweets and sauces.

UNUSUAL FRUITS

You can see some Caribbean fruits, such as bananas and pineapples in your local shops. But others are more unusual. Breadfruit has bumpy, pale-green skin and a creamy flesh. Ackee has an orange skin with a bright yellow fruit. It is the main ingredient of the national dish of Jamaica, ackee and saltfish.

▼ The climate of the Caribbean means that tropical fruits like pineapples and watermelons grow all year round.

▲ Breadfruit trees can grow as tall as 18 metres high! Although breadfruit is a fruit, it is often cooked like a vegetable and used instead of potatoes or rice.

▼ Vegetables in the Caribbean come in all kinds of shapes, sizes and colours.

Vegetables

Lots of different vegetables grow in the Caribbean. Many of the islanders grow vegetables just for themselves, but much is sold abroad.

Vegetables are cooked in hundreds of different ways. Caribbean cooks often mix both sweet and savoury ingredients in their food. Sweet potatoes are sometimes cooked in sugar (see recipe on page 19), or mashed. Yams are cooked like potatoes. Cassava can be made into a kind of flour, or eaten as a vegetable. Callaloo is like spinach and is used in a dish called pepperpot soup.

▲ Barbecued fish.

▼ Fishing is an important industry in the Caribbean.

Seafood

People in the Caribbean can choose from fish such as clams, lobster, tuna, snapper, shark, conch and mullet. Fish and seafood is used in festival foods, as well as everyday dishes. It is barbecued, curried or cooked in the traditional Caribbean style of 'jerk'. Jerk fish, beef or chicken is made by flavouring the fish or meat with a peppery sauce and then barbecuing it.

◀ Brightly coloured spices are bought by weight from open-air markets and shops throughout the Caribbean.

Spices

Wherever you go in the Caribbean, spices are usually used to flavour food. The mixture of spices varies from island to island. In Trinidad, people use *massala* in their dishes. This is a mixture of coriander seeds, anise, cloves, cumin, fenugreek, peppercorns, mustard and turmeric. Peppers are one of the most famous spices used in Caribbean cookery. Pepper sauces are made from hot, yellow peppers that grow all over the islands, and each cook has a different way of preparing the sauce.

HISTORY THROUGH FOOD

Caribbean dishes can tell you about the history of the islands. For example, *foo-foo, coo-coo* and *dunckunoo* (dishes made from plantain and okra) came from West Africa. Escovitched fish (marinated fish) is found in islands that were Spanish colonies, and *fricassee de poulet au coco* (chicken in coconut milk) is cooked on islands that were French.

11

Caribbean Religions

There are many different religions in the Caribbean. Most people are Christians – mainly Roman Catholics or Anglicans. There are also many people that follow versions of African religions, such as Voodoo, Pocomania and Santeria. In the Caribbean, however, these religions have been mixed with Christianity. In some countries, like Guyana and Trinidad, the Hindu and Muslim religions are also very popular.

▲ During the Santeria festival of Shango, beautifully prepared food is laid out on an altar as a religious offering.

◄ For Christians at this church in Barbados, the visit to church is a social as well as religious time.

Festivals and food

The food and festivals of the Caribbean reflect the many different religions and cultures there. A festival might be a celebration of a Muslim tradition, such as Id-ul-Fitr, which marks the end of Ramadan. But the food that is served can be any style, from Chinese to Brazilian! The one thing that all Caribbean cooking uses is fresh ingredients.

RASTAFARIANISM

In Jamaica there is a religion called Rastafarianism, which does not allow its followers to eat pork meat or fish without scales. Many Rastafarians are vegetarian or vegan. *Ital* food is a vegetarian type of cooking introduced by Rastafarians. It includes things like vegetable patties and it is now becoming popular in the Caribbean.

▲ This Rastafarian family in Jamaica wear the red, green and gold colours of their religion. The man is also wearing the dreadlock hairstyle that many Rastafarians wear.

▲ At this Hindu wedding in Trinidad, the bride is wearing a traditional red *sari*. Offerings of food, such as rice, are made to Hindu gods throughout the ceremony.

Food and celebrations

Food is an important part of most religious celebrations in the Caribbean. Voodoo followers, when asking for a favour from a spirit or 'Iwa', make offerings of cake and grilled corn. In a traditional Hindu wedding, only vegetarian food is served, but in Christian weddings it is common to eat meat dishes, such as curried lamb. There is a recipe for curried lamb on the opposite page.

◄ Curried lamb, with a selection of spices.

Curried Lamb

INGREDIENTS

30 g Olive oil

500 g Lamb, cut into cubes

2 Large onions, finely sliced

2 Teaspoons curry powder

1 Tablespoon freshly grated
   coconut or dessicated coconut

½ Teaspoon allspice

1 Lamb stock cube mixed in
   600 ml of water

1 Bay leaf

Pinch of cayenne pepper

Salt and a dash of Tabasco sauce

1 Ask an adult to heat the oil in the saucepan. Add the meat and fry for about 5 minutes. Take it out and put into a bowl.

2 In the same pan, fry the onions until soft. Stir in the curry powder, allspice and coconut and cook for a few minutes.

3 Add the lamb stock, bay leaf, cayenne pepper and the fried meat. Cover and simmer for 2 hours.

4 Taste and add more salt if needed. If using Tabasco sauce, stir in just before serving.

Be careful when frying. Ask an adult to help you.

Christmas and New Year

Christmas and New Year are celebrated all over the Caribbean. This is the season of bamboo bursting, when bamboo poles are filled with gunpowder and snapped, to sound like firecrackers. Lots of special dishes are prepared.

▼ Many of the traditions of Christmas that we know in Britain, such as Santa Claus, are also popular in the Caribbean.

Ham, turkey or a whole roasted pig or goat are some of the traditional Christmas foods served on many of the islands. Caribbean people also eat a Christmas cake very similar to the British one, but flavoured with rum.

SCOTTISH FOOD

Another European Christmas recipe is *jug jug*, which is a kind of pastie made from pork and beef. It is said to have come from Scotland originally.

Professional dancers in the ▶ Caribbean putting on a traditional dance for tourists. Dancing is an important part of Christmas celebrations.

17

Jonkonnu and Papa Jab

Christmas and New Year are also marked by parades. Pipes, cowbells, whistles, foghorns and drums, announce the arrival of the Jonkonnu (or John Canoe) dancers. The dancers are dressed in different costumes as animals, kings and funny characters, and their dancing pattern tells stories that have been passed down from one generation to the next.

Papa Jab is a folk character from St Lucia. During the New Year celebrations, someone dresses up as Papa Jab and joins groups of people in masks and costumes, singing and dancing through the streets. Children are scared of Papa Jab because legend has it that he will eat badly behaved children!

▲ Candied sweet potatoes is a favourite savoury dish in the Caribbean. There is a recipe for this dish on the opposite page.

HAPPY NEW YEAR

In Jamaica, there is a belief that to make sure you have a good year, the first thing that you eat in the New Year should be roasted suckling pig.

Candied Sweet Potatoes

INGREDIENTS

4 Sweet potatoes, peeled
Peel of 1 orange, grated
25 g Butter
3 Tablespoons brown sugar
1 Cup of water

EQUIPMENT

2 Saucepans   Baking dish, greased
Chopping board   Colander
Wooden spoon   Oven gloves
Knife

Turn the oven on to a medium temperature. Ask an adult to boil the potatoes for about 10 minutes. Drain and leave to cool. Cut into thick slices.

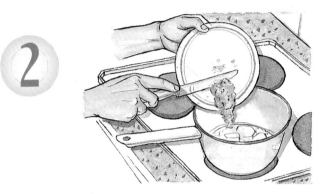

Put the orange peel in the second saucepan with the butter, sugar and water. Cook over a low flame, stirring constantly for 5 minutes, or until the sugar has melted and the mixture has thickened.

Arrange the sweet potatoes in the baking dish. Pour the orange syrup over them, making sure they are all coated evenly.

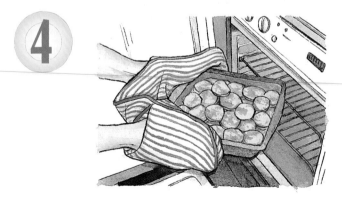

Put the dish in the oven and bake for 30 minutes or until browned. Ask an adult to take the potatoes out of the oven.

Always use oven gloves to take hot dishes from ovens. Ask an adult to help you.

19

Children's Carnival

In Trinidad and Tobago there is a children's carnival, which is just as colourful and exciting as the main carnival. Children dance and take part in competitions to see who is wearing the best costume.

▲ Children love taking part in the Carnival because it's a good opportunity for singing, dancing and having fun.

24

Fried Chicken

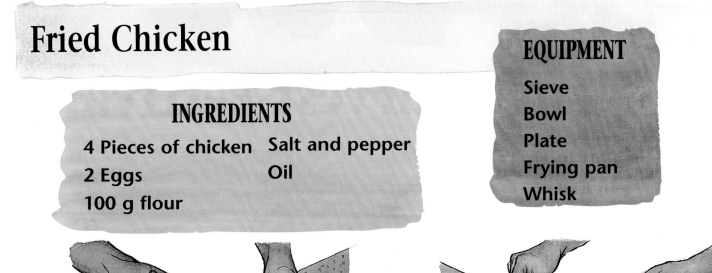

INGREDIENTS

4 Pieces of chicken   Salt and pepper

2 Eggs   Oil

100 g flour

EQUIPMENT

Sieve

Bowl

Plate

Frying pan

Whisk

Crack the eggs into a bowl and beat them well.

Add a pinch of salt and pepper to the flour and then sieve the mixture on to the plate.

Dip each of the chicken pieces into the beaten egg. Then roll them in the flour. Ask an adult to heat up enough oil in a frying pan to cover the chicken completely.

Once the oil is hot, add the chicken pieces one by one. Cook until they are brown on the outside and white on the inside.

Ask an adult to do the frying. Hot oil can be very dangerous.

Glossary

Anglican   One of the beliefs within the Church of England.

Ash Wednesday   The first day of Lent.

Calypso   A type of song that comes from the West Indies.

Christians   People who believe in Jesus Christ.

Colonisers   People who settle together in other countries.

Cuttings   Pieces cut from a plant.

Fasting   To give up eating and drinking.

Fertile   Land that is good for growing crops.

Hinduism   A major Indian religion, which is based on the belief that God has many forms.

Hurricanes   Very strong storms, which cause a lot of damage.

Id-ul-fitr   A Muslim ceremony which marks the end of Ramadan.

Mocko Jumbies   Dancers from Saint Thomas, who stand on stilts that make them 6 metres high.

Muslim   Somebody who follows the Islamic religion, who believes in one God, Allah.

Rastafarianism   A religion from Jamaica, which involves the worship of the old emperor of Ethiopia, Ras Tafari, as God.

Roman Catholicism   The Christian Church that is led by the Pope.

Rotis   Flat, Indian bread.

Sari   A piece of clothing from India. It is a long piece of cloth that is wrapped around the body like a dress and worn by women.

Vegan   Somebody who does not eat meat, fish or any animal products such as dairy products.

Vegetarian   Somebody who does not eat meat or fish.

Topic Web and Resources

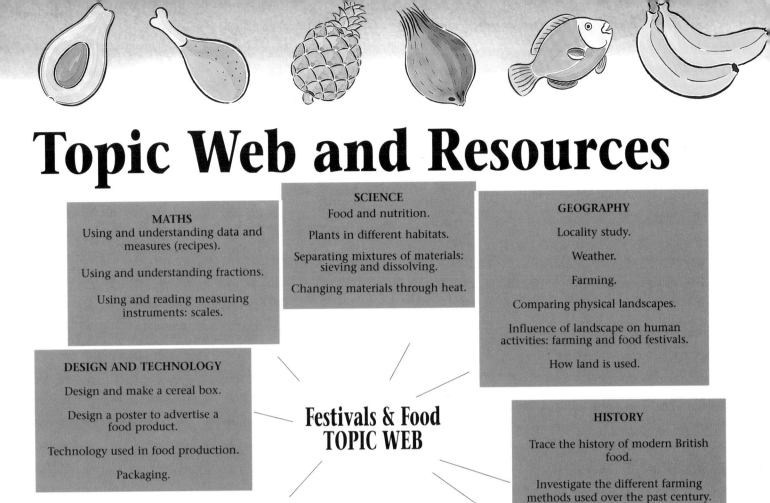

Festivals & Food TOPIC WEB

MATHS
Using and understanding data and measures (recipes).

Using and understanding fractions.

Using and reading measuring instruments: scales.

SCIENCE
Food and nutrition.

Plants in different habitats.

Separating mixtures of materials: sieving and dissolving.

Changing materials through heat.

GEOGRAPHY
Locality study.

Weather.

Farming.

Comparing physical landscapes.

Influence of landscape on human activities: farming and food festivals.

How land is used.

DESIGN AND TECHNOLOGY
Design and make a cereal box.

Design a poster to advertise a food product.

Technology used in food production.

Packaging.

HISTORY
Trace the history of modern British food.

Investigate the different farming methods used over the past century.

ENGLISH
Make up a slogan to sell a food product.

Write a poem or story using food as the subject.

Write a list of food words and non-food words.

Write a menu you might find in a Caribbean restaurant.

MODERN FOREIGN LANGUAGES
Language skills.

Everyday activities: food.

People, places and customs.

OTHER BOOKS TO READ

A World of Recipes: The Caribbean by Julie McCulloch (Heinemann Library, 2002)

Discover Other Cultures: Festivals Around The World by Meryl Doney (Franklin Watts, 2002)

Facts About Countries: The Caribbean by Ian Graham (Franklin Watts, 2005)

From the Heart of the Caribbean: The People of St Lucia by Alison Brownlie Bojang (Hodder Wayland, 2001)

Special Ceremonies: Feasts and Fasting by Cath Senker (Franklin Watts, 2005)

This book meets the following specific objectives of the National Literacy Strategy's Framework for Teaching:

 Range of work in non-fiction: simple recipes (Year 2, Term 1 & Year 3 Term 2), instructions, labels, captions, lists, glossary, index.

 Vocabulary extension: words linked to particular topics (food words) and technical words from work in other subjects (geography and food science).

Index

Page numbers in **bold** mean there is a photograph on the page.